D0819762

# The Easter Book

**Written and planned by**
Jenny Vaughan

**Managing Editor**
Mary Tapissier

**Production**
Jackie Fox

**Cover Illustration**
Barbara Bailey

**Illustrators**
Peter Dennis
pages 10-11, 12-13, 14-15, 18-19,
22-23 (top), 26-27, 30-31, 32-33,
36-37, 38, 39, 42-43
Sara Cole
8-9, 16-17, 22-23 (bottom), 24-25,
28-29, 34-35, 40-41
Joanna Troughton
4-5, 6-7, 20-21, 44-45, 46

**Poems**
pages 14-15, Breaking the Ice,
© Richard Blythe 1980
page 39, Spring,
Gerard Manley Hopkins
page 39, The Donkey, G. K. Chesterton
© The estate of the late G. K.
Chesterton and J. M. Dent Ltd.

**Advisory panel**
Sylvia Collicott, teacher
Pat Pronger, teacher

**Consultant on religion**
Desmond Brennan

**Ideas from**
Kate Hague, Peter Mansfield

**Song**
pages 42-32, Bunnies and Bonnets and
Hot Cross Buns, © Elizabeth Bennett
and Gordon Snell 1980

First published 1980
Macdonald Educational Ltd.

© Macdonald Educational Ltd 1980

First U.S. Printing 1981
All rights reserved.
Published simultaneously in Canada.
Published in the United States
by Grosset & Dunlap, Inc.

ISBN: 0-448-11541-7 (Trade Edition)
ISBN: 0-448-13492-6 (Library Edition)

Library of Congress Catalog Card No. 80-83362

Printed in the United States of America.

# The Easter Book

Publishers · GROSSET & DUNLAP · New York
A FILMWAYS COMPANY

# Contents

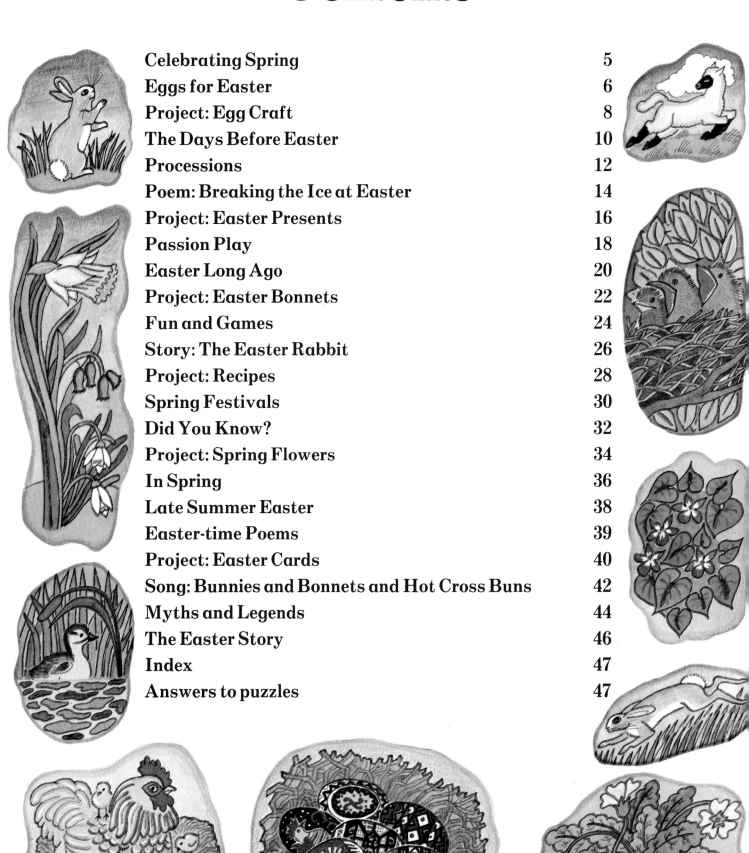

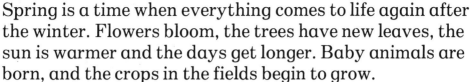

# Celebrating Spring

Spring is a time when everything comes to life again after the winter. Flowers bloom, the trees have new leaves, the sun is warmer and the days get longer. Baby animals are born, and the crops in the fields begin to grow.

Our ancestors were even more pleased to see the spring than we are. Winter was very hard for them. Their houses were cold, and people often had almost no food left by the time spring arrived. They were so glad to see the end of winter that they had a special celebration.

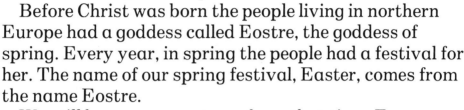

Before Christ was born the people living in northern Europe had a goddess called Eostre, the goddess of spring. Every year, in spring the people had a festival for her. The name of our spring festival, Easter, comes from the name Eostre.

We still keep some customs from that time. For example, in those days people cooked special cakes for the festival, rather like hot cross buns of today.

The Easter we know is a Christian festival. It is a time when people remember the story of how Jesus was killed and rose again from the dead. This happened in spring, so Christians celebrate at this time of year.

Since then, many spring celebrations have become part of Easter. The Greeks and many other people in the ancient world kept religious customs in spring. When they became Christians, they carried on with these making them into Easter traditions which they still keep, such as lighting special fires and candles.

Eggs are a special symbol of Easter in many countries of the world. It is easy to see why. An egg hatches into a baby bird, so it makes a symbol for the new life that comes to the world at springtime.

# Eggs for Easter

The custom of giving eggs at Easter is very old. The first Easter eggs were just ordinary hard-boiled eggs, painted or dyed. In some places in the north of England this is still done.

In Germany, there is a tradition that green eggs are eaten on the Thursday before Easter. The people dye the eggs by boiling them with spinach.

In Greece, people used to dye eggs red for Easter, but now they dye them all colors. The eggs are used in a special Easter greeting. Each person carries an egg, and when two people meet they knock the eggs together, saying "Christ is risen."

In some countries, children play a game, a bit like the British game of conkers, using hard-boiled eggs. They use painted eggs. Each of two players holds an egg in his right hand, and knocks the pointed ends together. The idea of the game is to crack the other person's egg first. The winner is the person whose egg has cracked the most others, but has not cracked itself.

Egg rolling is another old Easter game. Children roll eggs down a grassy slope. They do it to see whose gets to the bottom first, or to try to hit other eggs.

In Britain, the most famous egg rolling is in Preston in Lancashire. In America, an egg-rolling competition is held every year on the lawn of the President's house, the White House in Washington.

In many countries, the children get up very early on Easter Day and hunt for eggs, which their parents have hidden in the house and garden. The eggs are usually chocolate, but they used to be dyed or painted.

Sometimes the children make a special nest in the garden for the eggs. There is a story that the Easter Rabbit comes in the night and leaves the Easter eggs. He is sometimes called the Easter Bunny.

In many countries, roast lamb is eaten as a special Easter meal. In Greece, the lamb is roasted on a spit, and the Italians make a salad with hard-boiled eggs to eat with it.

There are many different kinds of Easter cakes too, especially in Italy and Germany. There are some recipes for Easter food on pages 28 and 29 of this book.

Greek cake
with a
dyed egg

Egg knocking game

Decorated eggs

# Egg Craft

You might like to make your own decorated eggs for Easter. Here are some ideas. You should use hard-boiled eggs for most of them. If you want to eat the eggs later, use vegetable dyes like onion or beetroot. Dot not varnish eggs you want to eat. You can make them shine by rubbing them with a little vegetable oil.

You can make a hollow egg by blowing the inside out. To do this you must use an egg that has been in a warm room for a few hours, and not one that has just come out of the refrigerator and is very cold.

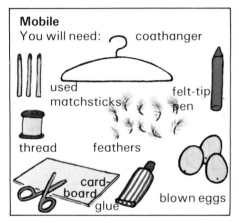

**Mobile**
You will need: coathanger, used matchsticks, felt-tip pen, thread, feathers, card-board, scissors, glue, blown eggs

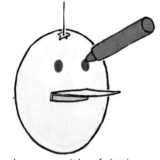

Tie a match to a thread and put it inside an egg.

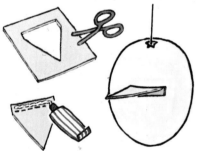

Cut out a beak shape. Fold and glue it, as the picture shows. Stick it on to the egg, like this.

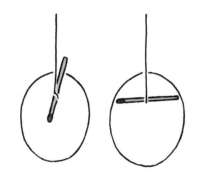

Draw in the eyes with a felt-tip pen. Make them big.

Glue two feathers onto each egg. These make the wings.

Hang the birds from the coathanger. Make sure they balance nicely.

## How to blow an egg

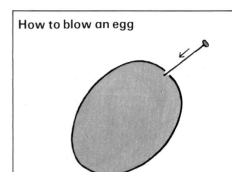

Prick the big end with a pin.

Make the hole bigger by chipping away the shell.

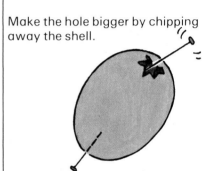

Make a hole in the small end. Put your fingers over each hole and shake the egg hard to break the yolk.

Blow through the small hole and empty the egg into a bowl.

Let the shell dry out.

Remember! The eggs must be room temperature or you will not be able to blow them.

## Dyes

spinach    onion

beetroot

tea

vinegar (for fixing)

Boil the onion skin for half an hour.

Sieve the skins and let the water cool. Put the eggs in and boil them until they are a good color. Add a few drops of vinegar, to fix the dye.

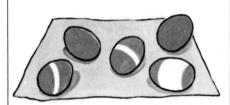

Drain and dry the eggs.

You can make the eggs patterned by using masking tape before you dye them.

## Wax-pattern egg
You will need:

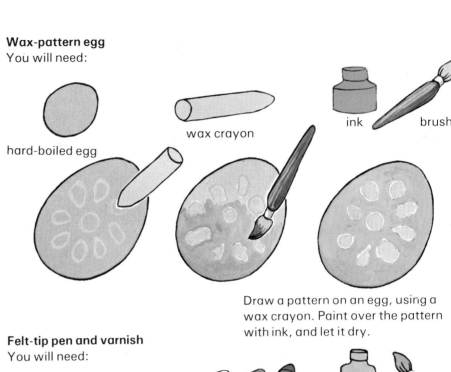

hard-boiled egg    wax crayon    ink    brush

Draw a pattern on an egg, using a wax crayon. Paint over the pattern with ink, and let it dry.

## Felt-tip pen and varnish
You will need:

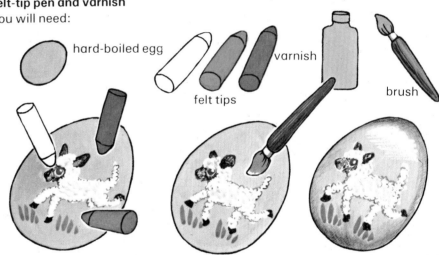

hard-boiled egg    felt tips    varnish    brush

Draw a picture, and then varnish the egg. Do the top part first. Let it dry, and then do the bottom half.

## Criss-cross egg
You will need:

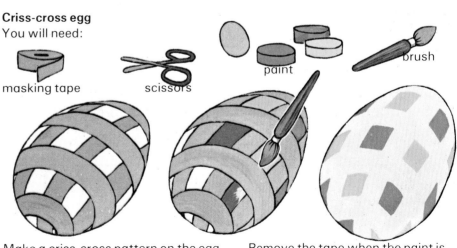

masking tape    scissors    paint    brush

Make a criss-cross pattern on the egg, using masking tape. Paint over it.

Remove the tape when the paint is dry, and you should have a pattern.

# The Days Before Easter

Pancake races are held on Shrove Tuesday.

Every Maundy Thursday, the Queen gives special money in colored leather purses to a group of pensioners. There is one pensioner for each year of the Queen's life. Some years this happens at Westminster Abbey, and at other times in a cathedral outside London. The custom started long ago when the king or queen used to give food and clothes to the poor and wash their feet. This was in memory of the time when Jesus washed his disciples' feet at the Last Supper.

Easter does not fall on the same date every year, like Christmas. Instead, it changes from year to year, depending on the time of the full moon in March. There are other festivals connected with Easter, and these change their date from year to year too.

Before the Easter celebrations begin, there is a fast called Lent. A fast is a time when people do not eat much. Lent is kept in memory of the story that Jesus fasted for 40 days in the wilderness.

Once, people were not allowed to eat eggs or fat during Lent. Making pancakes was a good way of using these up, and people still eat these the day before Lent. In some countries, there are carnivals and parties on this day. In England it is called Shrove Tuesday. Shrove comes from an old word for forgiven. In France it is called Mardi Gras or Fat Tuesday.

Ash Wednesday is the first day of Lent, when kings used to cover their heads with ashes to show they were sorry for the wrong things they had done. In some countries people smear their foreheads with ashes.

March 17th is Saint Patrick's Day. Saint Patrick is the patron saint of Ireland. There are many stories about him. One is that he drove all the snakes in Ireland into the sea. To this day, there are no snakes in Ireland.

The week before Easter is called Holy Week. It starts with Palm Sunday, when Christians remember the story of Jesus riding into Jerusalem on a donkey, and how people waved palm leaves and called him king.
In some churches, palm crosses are given. Next year, these are burned to make ashes for Ash Wednesday.

The Thursday of this week is Maundy Thursday. The story is that on this day, Jesus ate a last meal with his friends and told them that he was giving them a new rule to keep, that they should love one another. The name Maundy comes from an old word for "I give."

The Friday is called Good Friday. On this day, people remember that Jesus was killed.

The Sunday is the day when Christians believe that Jesus rose from the dead. It is the most important festival of the Christian year.

In England, the Sunday in the middle of Lent is called Mothering Sunday. It was once the time when people working away from home returned to see their families. Now it is a day when children are especially helpful to their mothers.

Simnel cake is the traditional cake for Mothering Sunday. Some people say that it must not be eaten until Easter.

Saint Valentine's day is on February 14th. People say this is the time when the birds choose their mates.

Shrove Tuesday is not only a time for pancakes. In many countries there are carnivals and parties. This carnival is in Trinidad in the West Indies.

# Processions

Easter is a time when many Christians hold processions. These are often on Palm Sunday. In Italy, they carry olive branches on this day, instead of palms, and in some countries pussy willow is used.

In parts of Germany, the priest used to ride to church on a donkey.

In some cities in Spain, there is a procession every evening of Holy Week. The most famous places where this happens are the towns of Seville and Vallaladoid.

There, huge platforms called *pasos* with statues of Jesus and Mary his mother are carried through the streets. Some pasos weigh about half a ton, and have to be carried by about 36 men. The procession goes through the streets for many hours and the men, hidden under a curtain which hangs around the bottom of each paso, get very hot and tired.

Men dressed in black hoods walk beside the pasos and others follow, with chains around their feet to show they are sorry for wrong things they have done.

The people of Mexico and parts of South America have similar processions. This is because the Spanish conquered parts of South America and introduced their customs to the people there.

In Jerusalem, processions are held along the roads where Jesus himself walked. First there is a Palm Sunday procession, and then, on Good Friday there is a procession along the road Jesus took to the place where he was to be executed. People take the parts of Jesus, the other men who were being executed and soldiers. The road they take is called the Via Dolorosa, or the sorrowful road.

The Palm Sunday procession in Jerusalem.

Easter week in Spain,
in the town of
Vallaladoid.

# Breaking the Ice at Easter

The winter has no pity
On a silent northern city,
  When you can't hear what is spoken
  And the words they say are frozen,
Falling solid from their lips.

But wait until it's Easter,
When it's warm, or when at least a
  Breath of air is not so bitter,
  And a thaw begins the pitter
And the patter of the drips.

For out run all the people,
And the bells rock every steeple,
  And the sun goes dancing higher
  As they light their Easter fire
To unfreeze their frozen lips.

by Richard Blythe

When Easter ends the winter,
Icy talk begins to splinter,
   And the lumpy words go runny;
   But it's not so very funny
To be deafened all to bits.

For silence turns to babble
As their words thaw out and gabble,
   From a patter to a clatter,
   Filling streets with melting chatter
From their winter's tales and quips.

Then springtime has no pity
On that noisy Easter city,
   For you can't hear what you utter
   When the place is all a-clutter
With what froze on winter's lips.

# Easter Presents

In Germany and Sweden and some other countries people decorate small branches and twigs at Easter.

In Germany, they use willow branches. They decorate these with ribbons, blown out painted eggs and pretzels, which are a kind of biscuit, made in a knot shape.

In Sweden, they use birch branches and decorate them with colored feathers. The pictures show you how to do this. You must use inks to dye the feathers, as paint will not stick.

You may need help to cut the wire and to fix it tightly

**Nest of eggs**
You will need:

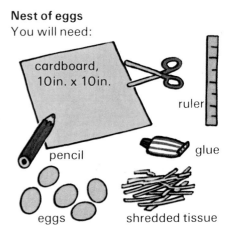

cardboard, 10in. x 10in.

pencil

ruler

glue

eggs

shredded tissue

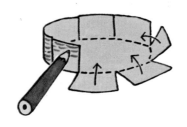

Draw two circles like these. Draw four lines through the center to the edges. Cut them like this.

Fold the cut edges up like this and tape them together.
Decorate the outside of the basket.

Fill the basket with shredded tissue paper and put in Easter eggs.

---

**Giant papier mâché egg**
You will need:

balloon

varnish

paste

paper

knife

paint

brush

lace

Blow the balloon up. Cover it with papier mâché. Let it dry out. Use a sharp knife to cut the balloon in half. You may need some help. Be very careful! Now paint and varnish the egg, and put Easter presents inside.

---

**Donkey carrier**
You will need:

wool

pieces of toilet roll tube

glue

cardboard

crayons

scissors

tape

2 eggs

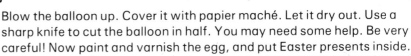

Fold the cardboard in half. Draw a donkey shape like this. Cut through both halves of the cardboard, but leave the top joined.

Join the two halves of the donkey's nose together, using glue. Do the same for the tail. Paste on the mane and the carriers, and put the eggs in.

**Birch twigs**
You will need:

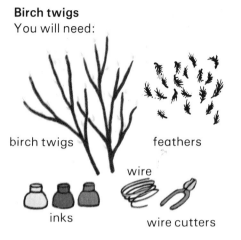

birch twigs

feathers

wire

inks

wire cutters

onto the twig without cutting into the stem.

Use a twig with buds on it, which you can pick and decorate a few days before Easter. Put it in water and wait for the leaves to come out.

Most of the things on this page are easy to make. You may need some help with the giant Easter egg, if you want to cut it in half. Ask a grown-up to do this, using a very sharp knife.

Line it with a paper doily or a piece of fabric and put sweets, or an Easter present inside.

Dye the feathers different colors, using inks. Let them dry out.

Attach the feathers to the twigs, using wire and wire cutters.

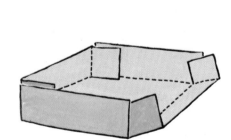

Put the twigs in water for a few days. Soon the leaves will come out.

**Bunny basket**
You will need

2 squares of cardboard, 8in. x 8in.

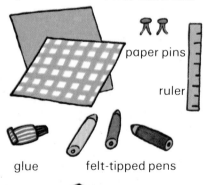

paper pins

ruler

glue

felt-tipped pens

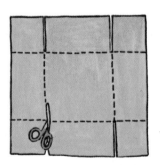

Cut the square in four places. Fold along the dotted lines and make X marks as the picture shows.

Fold up the sides to make the basket. Stick the corner flaps inside the walls of the basket.

Fold the other cardboard in half and draw a rabbit shape like this. Cut it out.

Fix a rabbit over each X mark. Join the rabbits at the ears. Stick a cotton wool tail on, over the pin.

Fill the bunny basket with tissue paper and put in the eggs. This makes a good Easter present.

17

# Passion Play

Oberammergau is a village in Germany. Every ten years, the people of the village perform a play about the life and death of Jesus. This sort of play is called a passion play. The one in Oberammergau is very famous.

The play has been put on every ten years for over 300 years. The first one was acted after there had been an outbreak of a very dangerous disease all over Europe. The disease was called the Black Death, or the plague. It is carried by the fleas of black rats. Hardly anybody catches it nowadays, but at that time many people died. Because no one knew how the disease spread, the people were very frightened of it.

The villagers of Oberammergau made a vow.

They promised that if the Black Death did not reach their village, they would show God how thankful they were by acting a passion play every ten years. No one caught the Black Death, so the first play was acted.

Visitors from all over the world come to see the play. A special outdoor theater has been built. It is huge. You can see part of it in the picture.

The play is performed twice a week, all summer.

All the people who act in the play come from the village of Oberammergau. A year before the play is put on they start to let their hair grow long. The men let their beards grow.

The only person who does not grow his hair long in the play is the man playing Pontius Pilate.

The country where Jesus lived, now called Israel, was part of the Roman empire. Pilate was the Roman Governor, and Romans had short hair and no beards. The part of Jesus' mother Mary is always played by an unmarried woman.

The story of how Jesus was killed tells us that he had to carry the heavy cross through Jerusalem, to the place where he was to be executed.

On his head he wore a crown made of thorns the soldiers had made. Later a man called Simon who was in the crowd helped Jesus with the cross.

Two other men were going to be executed in the same place. They were both thieves, and also carried their crosses. The picture shows this scene from the play.

# Easter Long Ago

Easter used to be much more of a celebration than it is now. The fast of Lent went on for 40 days, and the people really looked forward to a time when they could enjoy themselves.

Sometimes in England the whole village had a big feast together. The vicar often had to pay for it!

Because no one was allowed to eat eggs in Lent, people liked to eat plenty of them on Easter Sunday. Children used to go from house to house, singing and begging for eggs. They were paid in hard-boiled eggs, dyed with vegetables like the ones shown on page 9.

The eggs were called pace eggs. The word pace comes from the French *Pasque*, which means Easter.

People used to light bonfires on Easter Day. Sometimes they would either burn or drown a straw doll. The doll was a symbol of winter.

In some places, people used to put all their fires out the day before Easter. In the evening the priest lit a special bonfire and the people used to relight their own fires using logs and sticks from the Easter fire. In some churches an Easter fire is still made, and the candles for the church are lit from this fire.

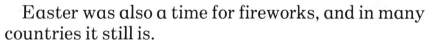
New clothes for Easter

The Easter Rabbit

Lifting or heaving

Easter was also a time for fireworks, and in many countries it still is.

In Sweden, people used to say that the fireworks would frighten off the witches. Children dressed up as witches at Easter. The picture shows this, many years ago.

In England, there was an old custom called lifting or heaving. On Easter Monday, the men in a village would go from house to house and lift up the women.

The next day, it was the women's turn to lift the men. In some parts of Europe the girls used to hang a swing on a cherry tree at Easter time.

Another old custom was to wear new clothes on Easter Sunday. People thought that if you could afford these, and did not wear them, you would have bad luck.

The tradition of the Easter Rabbit is very old. People used to sacrifice hares to the goddess of Eostre. There were hare hunts at this time.

Now the hare is still part of Easter, but no one thinks it is sacred any more. It is a magical hare or rabbit that brings eggs to children. It is the Easter Bunny.

# Easter Bonnets

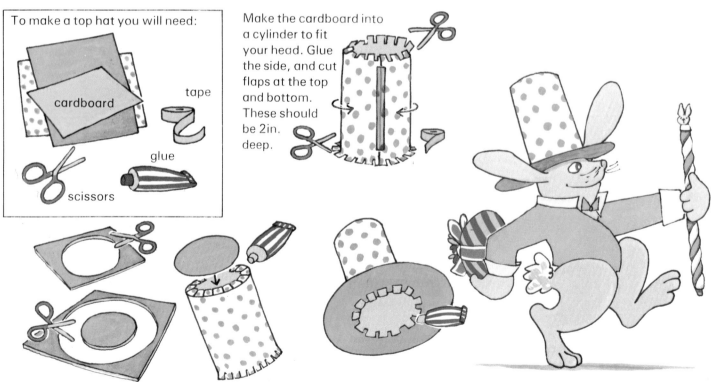

To make a top hat you will need:

cardboard

tape

glue

scissors

Make the cardboard into a cylinder to fit your head. Glue the side, and cut flaps at the top and bottom. These should be 2in. deep.

Make a brim. Cut a hole in the brim for your head. Use the cylinder as a pattern to get the size right.

Cut a top for the hat. Use the cylinder you have made as a pattern. Fix the top on with glue.

Push the hat through the hole. Glue the brim on and decorate your hat.

In some towns and cities there is a big parade on Easter Sunday, with an Easter bonnet competition when people wear funny hats. These are often ones they have made themselves.

The idea comes from the time when it was the custom to wear new clothes on Easter Day.

Perhaps you could arrange an Easter parade and a bonnet competition with your friends.

See if you can make an Easter hat for yourself. The pictures show you how to make the shapes for a bonnet, or a hat, but the decorations are up to you.

Or you could make something quite different. There is a story that a lady once turned up at an Easter parade wearing a hat just like a birdcage, with real birds in it!

To make an Easter bonnet you will need:

tape

cardboard

glue

scissors

ribbon

Bend the cardboard like this to make a brim and cut flaps 2in. deep.

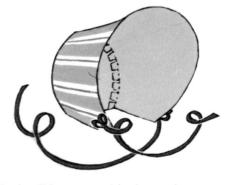

Cut out the bonnet back and fit it onto the brim. Stick the flaps on the inside.

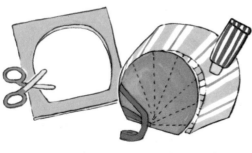

Fix the ribbons on with glue and decorate your hat.

Now you are ready for the Easter Parade. Good luck!

# Fun and Games

**Find the pairs of eggs**

Get the Easter Bunny
to the Easter eggs

## Rabbits and eggs
### A game for four players

Put your homemade counters face down and mix them up. Put them on the rabbit squares at the bottom of the page, still face down.

The aim of the game is to get all the colored rabbit counters to the same colored eggs at the top of the page, with one counter on each egg.

Each player throws the dice. The person with the highest score chooses a color and turns over the rabbits opposite it. The next highest scorer chooses another color and so on.

Now the game starts. Players take turns to throw the dice and move a counter of their chosen color, one square at a time, in any direction according to the number thrown. If one card lands on another, the one already there must go back to the start.

**Egg blowing game**
This is a game that people play on Easter Sunday in Germany. You need a blown egg. Look at page 8 to see how to make one.

The players must stand around the table and blow the egg to one another. They must not let it fall off the table.

# Rabbits and Eggs

Make 12 counters, using cardboard. Make them the right size to fit on the squares. The cards should all look the same on one side.

Draw a rabbit on the other side. Use four colors, so that you have three rabbits in each color.

# The Easter Bunny

Tom and Joanna liked to visit their grandmother. They used to go to her house every Thursday after school. They drank cocoa out of pretty teacups and ate freshly baked cookies.

When the weather was cold and gray they sat inside, all cozy and warm, and toasted their toes in front of the flickery flames of a roaring log fire. When the weather was fine and sunny they sat out in the garden.

Gran and the children played a game. They took turns telling a story every week. The children always thought that Gran's stories were the best.

The Friday before Easter, Tom and Joanna were on holiday from school. This Friday had a special name. It was called Good Friday. The children helped their mother and father on the farm most of the day. They collected the hens' eggs and cleaned out the rabbits' hutch and fed the pigs.

At half past three they changed into clean clothes and brushed their hair. It was time to go to Gran's. Mom had been busy in the farmhouse kitchen baking a fruit cake. It was an Easter present for Gran. She put it in a basket and gave it to the children to carry between them.

There was a large field between the farm and village of Honeysuckle Hill where Gran lived. The children climbed a fence to get into the field, and set off across the grass.

It was a lively afternoon for a walk. The sky was blue, and the weather was very warm for April. A very gentle breeze ruffled the new leaves on the tree. Dad's milking cows were grazing on the grass. They lifted their heads and gazed at the children with their soft brown eyes.

Suddenly, Tom Stopped and pointed ahead. "Look," he whispered, "there, near that mound of earth." Joanna shielded her eyes from the sun and looked. It was the biggest rabbit she had ever seen. It sat quite still on its haunches, watching them. Its ears were enormous, and stood straight up on top of its head. The children could just see its long whiskers.

Tom and Joanna walked forward with the basket dangling between them.

"It's sure to run away now," said Tom. But it did not move a step. It stayed in exactly the same place and stared at them. The children went closer and closer. The rabbit sat there.

"This is weird," said Joanna when they were only a few paces away. "Rabbits always run away when somebody comes."

"Perhaps it's a special sort of rabbit," replied Tom.

No sooner had he said this, than the rabbit bounded away. It reached the edge of the field and stopped. It turned and looked back at them.

When Tom and Joanna got to Gran's cottage they burst in the front door. "Guess what! We've just seen the hugest rabbit in the world and it didn't run away from us, not even when we went right up close to it," said Tom all in one breath.

"My goodness!" exclaimed Gran, taking the basket from them. "Well you had better come and tell me all about it. The cocoa and cookies are ready, and we have Mom's nice cake to eat too."

Tom and Joanna helped Gran set the table. Gran poured the cocoa while the children told her about the rabbit and helped themselves to cake.

"Well imagine that!" said Gran. "It must have been the Easter Bunny." Her eyes twinkled.

Tom looked puzzled. "What's the

by Liz Cooper

Easter Bunny?'' he asked.

"I'll tell you about him," Gran replied. "It's my turn for the story this week isn't it?''

The children nodded.

They listened while Gran told her story. It was about her when she was a little girl. Her mother had told her that if she made a nest for the Easter Bunny, it would come on Easter Day and leave some chocolate eggs for her. So she had gone into the garden and built a nest out of leaves and twigs and moss. Sure enough, there were eggs in it on Easter Day. They were made of chocolate and wrapped in gold paper.

On the way home from Gran's, Tom and Joanna decided that they would try making a nest for the Easter Bunny too.

"I think we should make the nest tomorrow morning after breakfast," said Tom.

Joanna agreed. "Yes," she said. "Then it will be ready in plenty of time for the Easter Bunny to come and leave his eggs on Sunday."

The next day was Saturday. Tom and Joanna had their breakfast early and went out into the farmyard.

"It will need to be quite a big nest for a rabbit, won't it?" said Joanna.

"Yes, it will," said Tom.

They collected a pile of twigs and leaves and moss, just as Gran had said, and put them on a large piece of light wire mesh. Then they wrapped the mesh around to make the shape of a nest with a hollow in the middle. To make a lining they got handfuls of mud and packed it over the wire mesh, smoothing it with their hands.

A few hours later, the mud was dry, and Tom and Joanna scattered some soft, downy duck feathers inside the nest. Dad stopped to have a look on his way from the tractor shed to the house. "That's a fine nest," he said.

"Who's it for?''

"The Easter Bunny," said Tom proudly.

"Oh, I see," said Dad. "Where are you going to put it?''

"Over there by the fence so that it's easy for the Easter Bunny to find," replied Joanna, "We saw him yesterday. He lives in the field where the cows are."

"Oh, does he indeed," said Dad. "I'll look forward to meeting him on Easter Day then."

Dad walked on up to the house. The children picked up the nest carefully and moved it to the fence. They put it a little to one side so that no one would step on it and settled it in a patch of long, thick grass.

It seemed years until Sunday morning.

At last it came. The children had to have their breakfast before they could go outside. Tom was so excited that he could only eat half a piece of toast, and hardly that.

At nine o'clock they rushed out into the farmyard and down to the fence. As they came around the corner of the chicken sheds they scarcely dared to look.

When they did, they stopped and stared.

They could hardly see the nest.

Sitting in it was their biggest hen, Penelope. She sat like a queen. Her head was held high and her feathers were fluffed up all around her.

"Penelope!" shouted Tom, crossly. "Get off. That's the Easter Bunny's nest."

Poor Penelope squawked and flapped and flew away.

"Well, we'll have to come back later," said Tom, heaving a big sigh.

"No we won't," said Joanna. "Look." In the nest were five eggs. One of them was Penelope's. The other four were wrapped in shiny gold paper. There was a note with them. It said: "HAPPY EASTER from the Easter Bunny".

The children jumped up on the fence and looked over into the field. An animal shot out of the long grass and raced across the field. Could it have been the Easter Bunny—watching?

27

# Recipes

Be sure to ask a grown-up for help when you use the stove or the oven.

## Easter cookies
You will need:

Oven: 180°C, 350°F

1 beaten egg
A little lemon juice and grated lemon rind
1 cup self-raising flour
½ cup butter or margarine
½ cup sugar
¼ cup currants or raisins
A pinch of salt

Mix the flour and the salt together. Rub in the fat, using the tips of your fingers. When it looks like breadcrumbs, add the sugar, the lemon rind, a teaspoon of lemon juice, and the beaten egg. Stir it all up then press it with your hands to make dough. Roll it out until it is about a ¼ inch thick and then cut it into shapes. You can use a cookie cutter in the shape of a rabbit. Put the cookies on a greased baking tray and bake them for 14 minutes in a warm oven. This makes 25-30 cookies.

---

## Hot cross buns
You will need:

Oven: 220°C, 425°F

⅓ oz yeast (or one level tablespoon of dried yeast)
¼ cup sugar, plus a teaspoonful for the yeast
1 teaspoon mixed spice and 1 of salt
1 cup warm milk
2 cups plain flour
1½ tablespoons lard or shortening
¼ cup raisins

You will also need to make a glaze by boiling two tablespoons of sugar with two of water. Do this when the buns are nearly ready, as you must put the hot glaze on after they are cooked.

    Add the teaspoonful of sugar to the milk. Stir it up, add the yeast. If you are using fresh yeast, crumble it first. If you use dried yeast, stir it into the milk for a few seconds using a whisk. Make sure the milk is warm, but not hot. If yeast gets too hot it does not work. Sprinkle a little flour on top of the milk and yeast mixture, and put it in a warm place for about 15 minutes, until it starts to look frothy. Again, do not let it get too hot.

Now turn the oven on. Put the rest of the flour in a warm bowl, mix the salt in and rub in the shortening. Then put in the sugar, the raisins and the mixed spice. Mix in the yeast and milk mixture to make a dough. You may need to add more milk.

Knead the dough well. This means you must push and stretch it on a floured board, roll it up and push and stretch it again. Do this for five or ten minutes.

Now roll it into a ball, cover it, and leave it for about 40 minutes, to rise. When it is twice the size it was, cut it into 12 pieces and gently shape each one into a bun. Put the buns on a greased tray, and use a knife to make the crosses.

Put them in the oven for about 20 minutes. Take them out and tap one on the bottom. If it sounds hollow, it is cooked. If not, put all the buns back for a few minutes. Paint the glaze onto the buns while they are hot.

---

## Italian Easter dove cake

You need some pieces of sponge cake large enough to cut into two dove shapes. You can make these using a sponge cake mix.
You will also need to make a dove-shaped pattern like the one in the picture. Use this to help cut the sponge cake.

You will also need:
1 carton whipping cream, sweetened
Fruit flavored syrup (used for putting on ice cream)
The white of an egg and some water
1 cup of confectioners' sugar
Whip the cream until it is stiff. Spread it over one dove shape, and put the other on top. Put the egg white into a bowl, beat it with a fork and add the sugar, a spoonful at a time. Before it gets stiff, add about three spoons of water, and enough syrup to make the mixture change color. Go on adding sugar until the mixture is nearly stiff then spread it over the top of the dove cake.

**The story of the dove cake**

Once, in Italy, there was a king who wanted to capture a city.

But his horse did not agree with him and would not gallop to battle.

The horse changed his mind when a girl offered him a cake like a dove, the bird of peace. Then the king changed his mind too, and decided not to conquer the city.

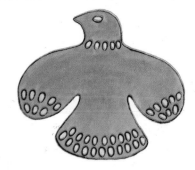

29

# Spring Festivals

People from India have a spring festival called Holi.

Holi is a happy time, when people who belong to the Hindu religion remember the story of how the god Krishna appeared, dancing and playing the flute. The festival is kept by the Indian people even when they are living in other countries,

People make special food and visit each other, tasting the food. It is the custom for the owner of the house to mark the guests' foreheads with colored powder.

Out in the street, people throw handfuls of the colored powder and then squirt water, so that the powder sticks. Men and women may throw mud at each other.

There are also processions, with people carrying statues of Krishna through the streets, and in the evening bonfires are lit.

The people who belong to the Sikh religion, which is also from India, have a festival very like Holi, called Hola. The names Holi and Hola come from the word *Holaka* which is rather like 'Alleluia', a word Christians use.

One of the most famous spring celebrations is the Jewish festival of the Passover.

This is the time when the Jewish people remember that their ancestors were once slaves in Egypt and were rescued by Moses, who led them to the country that is now called Israel.

Jewish familes have a special meal at Passover, to help them remember the story of how they left Egypt. The bread is flat and crisp, because they had to pack up in such a hurry that there was no time to let it rise.

They eat roast lamb with bitter herbs, as a sign of their troubles. There is a paste made from fruit and nuts to remind them of the clay bricks the slaves made. There is an egg, as a sign of the new life ahead.

It is the tradition for the youngest boy in the family to ask questions about the meal, and for the father to explain why Passover is so special.

In Japan, there is an important festival in spring, often called the Flower Festival. It is the birthday of Buddha, the founder of the Buddhist religion. The people decorate the temples with flowers, and make special scented tea to sprinkle around the temples.

People make bonfires . . .

and have mud fights

Washing off the colored dye.

# Did You Know?

The tradition of the Easter Egg Roll at the White House in Washington, D.C., was first begun by President Rutherford B. Hayes in 1878. Since then, the years between 1942 and 1953 have been the only years that this celebration did not take place.

On the Monday after Easter Sunday, all children who want to, may join the famous egg-rolling race — no special invitation is needed! But adults are only permitted to attend the event on the White House lawn if they're accompanied by a child.

Many Americans attend church services at sunrise on Easter morning. They gather outdoors in places such as the Hollywood Bowl in Hollywood, California, and the Punchbowl in Honolulu, Hawaii. In some towns, the singing of the choir calls people to church before dawn.

**Easter and springtime quiz**

1 Who was Eostre?

2 How did the tradition of the Easter Bunny begin?

3 What is the big event in Sydney at Easter time?

4 What happens if you stay in the churchyard all through the night before Saint Mark's Day?

5 Why are there no snakes in Ireland?

6 Which comes first, Maundy Thursday or Easter Sunday?

See page 47 for the numbers of the pages where you can find the answers.

**Springtime jokes**

Q Which side of the chicken had the most feathers?
A *The outside.*

Q How do you stop a rooster crowing on Monday morning?
A *Eat him for Sunday lunch.*

Q What did the Spanish farmer say to his chicken?
A *Olé.*

Q Who came second after the hare when the animals had a race?
A *A hot cross bun!*

These huge statues can be found on Easter Island, in the Pacific Ocean. No one really knows how they got there, but many experts think that they were built hundreds of years ago by people who came from South America. The Island got its name because it was discovered by Dutch sailors at Easter time in 1722.

There is a pub in East London called the Widow's Son. It is said to have been built on land where a widow's house once stood. The widow had a son who was a sailor. One Good Friday, when she was expecting her son to come home from sea, she baked him a hot cross bun. But he was shipwrecked. His mother always believed he would one day return and every year she baked another bun, but he never came back.

Every year the landlord of the pub asks a sailor to put a bun in a basket.

In Germany, there is a tradition that an egg laid on Good Friday will last for 100 years. But if you eat it at once it will make you very healthy.

Some people say that Good Friday is the best day for planting potatoes.

In Eastern Europe, there is a tradition that it is good luck to sprinkle water on people at Easter time. These people have dressed up in traditional costume for the game.

# Spring Flowers

Try growing some bulbs this spring. The pictures show you how to grow them in a bowl indoors. This makes the bulbs flower sooner in the year than they would if they were outside.

You can buy bulbs in the shops in autumn. Plant them in October or November, either indoors or out.

The first spring flowers are snowdrops and crocuses. Daffodils come later.

You could grow some spring flowers in a window box.

**Bulbs**
You will need:

bulbs

large bowl

bulb fibre

bucket

Put the fibre into the bucket. Fill the bucket with water and leave it overnight.

Next day, squeeze the water from the fibre and half fill the bowl.

Put the bulbs in the bowl.

Press them into the fibre and fill in the spaces with more squeezed fibre. Press it down firmly, but leave the tips showing.

Now put the bowl in a cupboard. It should be dark, but airy and cool. Leave the bulbs for two months. Keep the fibre moist, but not too wet.

Bring the bowl out into the warmth and sunlight. Keep the fibre moist, and soon the flowers will bloom.

Daffodils

Snowdrops

Crocuses

## Pressed flowers

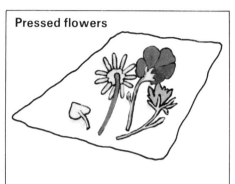

Put the flowers face down on blotting paper. Put another sheet on top.

Press the blotting paper and flowers with heavy books.

If you do that, you don't have to keep them in the dark. Just plant them outside, and when spring comes they will start to grow. You could grow polyanthus in the window-box. These are not bulbs but plants like primroses, and they come in many colors. It is easier to buy them from a garden shop as plants, not seeds.

If you want to press flowers, it is best to use some from a garden, or ones you have grown yourself. Don't use wild flowers as many of these are becoming rare. If too many people pick them, there will be none left.

### Daffodil
You will need: card, egg carton, pinking shears, yellow paint and green pipe cleaner.

Cut the cup of an egg box with pinking shears. Paint it yellow and let it dry.

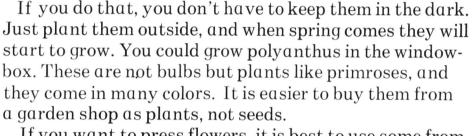

Cut the yellow card into petal shapes. Knot one end of the pipe cleaner and push it through the two bits of the flower, like this.

### Big flower

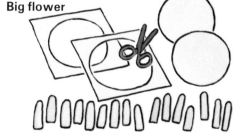

Cut two circles the same size and make petals.

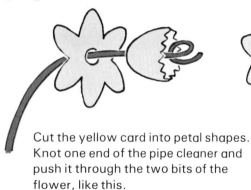

Stick the petals onto one circle, like this. Then stick the other circle on top.

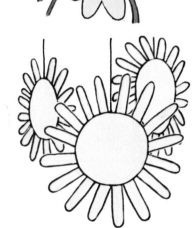

Hang the flowers from the ceiling, or use them to make a mobile.

# In Spring

As the weather gets warmer, young animals and birds are born. A male bird starts by choosing an area which is called his territory. It is as if the area belongs to him.

He will not allow any other male of the same kind into the territory. He will sing loudly and fluff up his feathers fiercely and drive off the male birds. At the same time he tries to attract a female to be his mate.

Once the male has chosen a female, nest building begins. You can help the birds to nest by putting nesting materials out on a bird table. You can put out wool, straw, and shreds of paper.

Once the nest is built, the female can lay her eggs. The eggs have to be kept warm and turned over regularly. Unless this happens, the baby birds will die. With some kinds of birds the male and female share the work of sitting on the eggs to keep them warm. Sometimes it is just the female.

If you find a nest, do not go too close or you may disturb the birds.

Many baby birds are helpless, and have no feathers, so the parents have to find food for them and keep them warm. Some, like chicks, can peck food almost at once, but they stay with their mother for safety.

Many plants flower in the spring. Look for daisies, dandelions and buttercups, as well as the flowers in the picture.

The insects wake up from their winter sleep, and bees and wasps start making new nests and laying eggs.

In the ponds, frogs and toads are also laying their eggs. These are called spawn. The babies are surrounded by jelly. Soon they grow into tadpoles, which eventually change into tiny frogs or toads.

This picture shows some of the things in the countryside in spring, but they do not all appear at once. You might see lambs in February, frogspawn in March, primroses in March and April, bluebells in April and May, baby rabbits, daffodils and cherry blossom in April, ducklings and hawthorn in May and swallows in May and June. Make your own list of what you see.

Start your list in February and keep working on it until the end of May or June.

# Late Summer Easter

In Australia, because the seasons are different, Easter comes at the end of summer instead of in spring.

The weather is still quite warm, and families like to go off to the country for a short holiday. The people in the picture are on a camping holiday.

In one of the biggest towns, Sydney, there is a big agricultural show called the Royal Easter Show. There are exhibitions of fruit and vegetables and homemade jams.

There is also a cattle show, a special kind of horse racing, show jumping, a cat show, children's art

ROYAL EASTER SHOW

I AM AN ARTIST

competitions, a funfair and many other kinds of exhibitions. The children buy bags of goodies from the stalls, go on rides at the fair and watch firework displays.

Out in the country, the fruit is growing ripe, and many farmers are busy.

Some European traditions have been taken to Australia by the people who have gone to live there. One of these is the Easter Bunny. People hide eggs in the garden for the children to find, just as they do in Europe.

# Easter-time Poems

### Spring

Nothing is so beautiful as Spring—
  When weeds, in wheels, shoot long and lovely and
    lush;
  Thrush's eggs look like little low heavens, and thrush
Through the echoing timber does so rinse and wring
The ear, it strikes like lightnings to hear him sing;
  The glassy peartree leaves and blooms, they brush
  The descending blue; that blue is all in a rush
With richness; the racing lambs too have fair their fling.

Gerard Manley Hopkins

### The Donkey

When fishes flew and forests walked,
  And figs grew upon thorn,
Some moments when the moon was
    blood,
  Then surely I was born;

With monstrous head and sickening cry
  And ears like errant wings,
The devil's walking parody
  On all four-footed things.

The tattered outlaw of the earth,
  Of ancient crooked will;
Starve, scourge, deride me; I am dumb,
  I keep my secret still.

Fools! For I also had my hour;
  One far fierce hour and sweet;
There was a shout about my ears,
  And palms before my feet.

G. K. Chesterton

39

# Easter Cards

Easter cards are fun to make. The traditional pictures are of rabbits, chicks and flowers.

These pictures will give you some ideas, but there are many more you can try. Silver paper can be very pretty. You could make a mosaic from pieces of eggshell stuck onto cardboard.

You can make a pop-up rabbit, like the chick. He can jump in and out of his burrow. Or he could be peeping over the grass.

Instead of using pressed flowers for a card, you could cut out pictures from magazines or seed catalogs. Cut out plenty, and stick them down in layers, so they make it look like a big bunch.

Try making a surprise card by sticking the bouquet inside the card and leaving the cover plain.

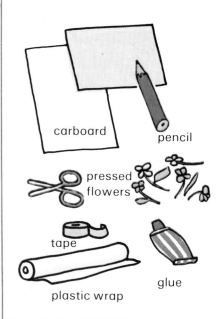

**Pressed flower card**
You will need:

carboard    pencil

pressed flowers

tape

plastic wrap    glue

**Hatching chick card**
You will need:

These two pictures show the sort of cards people living in Germany about a hundred years ago sent to their friends.

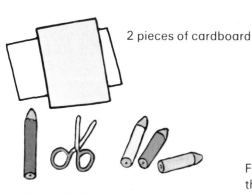

2 pieces of cardboard

pencil    scissors    crayons

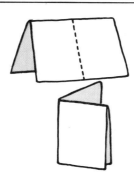

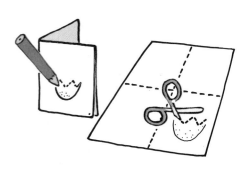

Fold a piece of cardboard, like this, and draw half an egg shape on it. Cut along the zig-zag edge of the egg, as the picture shows. You might find it easier to cut out a whole egg shape, cut it in half, and stick one half onto the cardboard.

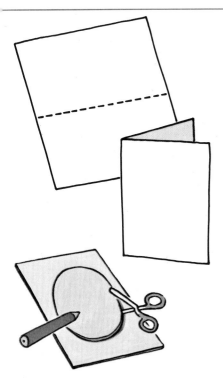

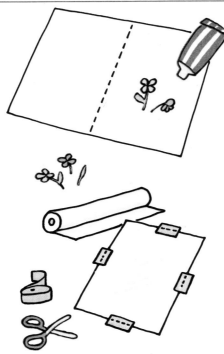

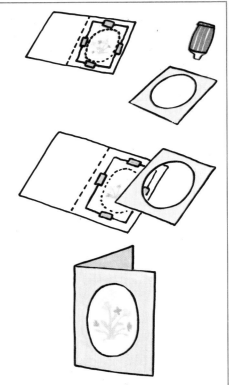

Fold the larger piece of cardboard in half. Cut the other piece to the same size as the front of the card, and carefully cut an oval from the center.

Stick the pressed flowers in a pattern on the front of the card. Make sure the pattern will fit into the oval shape. Cover the flowers with plastic wrap, held in place with tape.

Now stick the piece of card with the oval cut out over the plastic. Fold the card again, and stand it up.

## Cottontail card
You will need:

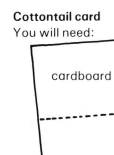

cardboard

3 cotton wool tails

glue

crayons

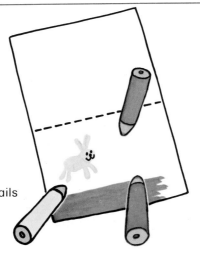

Draw a picture.

Stick on the tails.

Make a chick on a stalk like this. Stick a matching half of the egg on his head.

Push the chick through the slot in the front of the card.

Use the stalk as a lever to make the chick bob up and down.

# Bunnies and Bonnets...

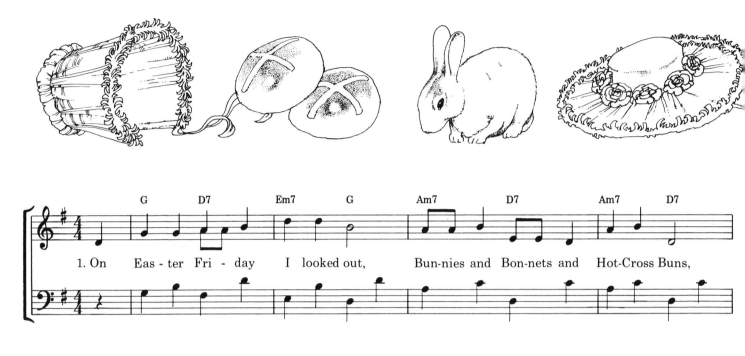

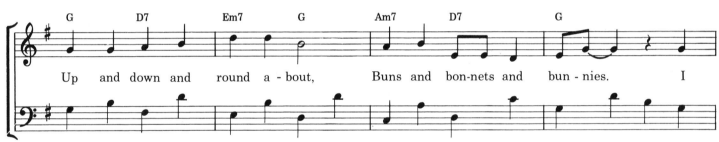

1. On Eas-ter Fri-day I looked out, Bun-nies and Bon-nets and Hot-Cross Buns,

Up and down and round a-bout, Buns and bon-nets and bun-nies. I

**2**

On Easter Saturday I looked out,
Bunnies and Bonnets and Hot-Cross Buns,
Up and down and round about,
Buns and bonnets and bunnies.

I saw a girl in fancy frills
Leaping up and down the hills
Waving seven daffodils,
On a Saturday morning.

**1**

On Easter Friday I looked out,
Bunnies and Bonnets and Hot-Cross Buns,
Up and down and round about,
Buns and bonnets and bunnies.

I saw a man hop on one leg
Dancing on a powder keg
Juggling with an Easter egg,
On a Friday morning.

# ...and Hot Cross Buns

© 1980 words: Gordon Snell, music: Elizabeth Bennett

saw a man hop on one leg, Dan - cing on a pow - der keg.

Jug - gling with an. Eas - ter Egg, On a Fri - day morn - ing.

**4**

On Easter Monday I looked out,
Bunnies and Bonnets and Hot-Cross Buns,
Up and down and round about,
Buns and bonnets and bunnies.

   I saw nine lambs with woolly tails
   In a boat with yellow sails
   Try to catch a shoal of whales
   On a Monday morning.

**3**

On Easter Sunday I looked out,
Bunnies and Bonnets and Hot-Cross Buns,
Up and down and round about,
Buns and bonnets and bunnies.

   I saw ten chicks and a big fat hen
   Dance a jig around the glen
   With a robin and a wren,
   On a Sunday morning.

43

# Myths and Legends

The myths and legends of Easter and spring are very old and very strange.

In some places the people believed that the sun danced on Easter morning, and that if you got up early and went to a high place you could see this, if the devil did not try to block your view.

There are stories that water has magical healing power at this time.

In parts of England there was a strange belief about Saint Mark's Eve. Saint Mark's Day falls on April 25th. The story was that if you went to the churchyard the night before, you would see all the people in the village who were going to die during the year, go into the church.

When Jesus died, he was put in a tomb in a garden belonging to a man called Joseph of Aramathea. There is a tradition that Joseph later went to Glastonbury, in Somerset. He traveled with a staff in his hand, and when he arrived he pushed it into the ground, where it grew into a flowering thorn tree.

There is still a thorn tree which flowers at Christmas

in the ruins of Glastonbury Abbey.

If you look at a donkey's back you will see that it has a mark like a cross on it. Some people say that the mark first appeared after Jesus rode into Jerusalem on the first Palm Sunday.

Long ago, the Greek people used to tell the story of how winter ends and spring arrives.

The earth-goddess Demeter, had a daughter called Persephone, who, while she was picking flowers in a field was stolen by the god Hades and carried off to his underground kingdom. Demeter was so sad that she let all the plants on the earth wither and die, and the earth grew cold.

At last she found Persephone, but was only able to have her back for half the year. This is summertime, when the flowers bloom.

In autumn, Persephone has to go back to Hades and then winter comes, because Demeter is so sad. Every spring Persephone returns to her mother who makes the earth come to life again.

# The Easter Story

This is the Christian Easter story.

Jesus lived almost two thousand years ago in a country called Judea. This land is now called Israel.

He preached a new kind of religion, and the leaders of the older religion thought he was dangerous, and might start a revolution.

One Sunday, Jesus rode into Jerusalem on a donkey. Crowds of people cheered him and called him king. Then he went to the temple, where, in those days, there were traders and money lenders. Jesus was very angry. He said that God's house was being made into a den of thieves. He tipped the stalls over and spilled the money everywhere.

His enemies were plotting to kill him, and they paid Judas, one of his friends to betray him.

It was the time of the Passover, and as Jesus was Jewish he wanted to celebrate this feast.

On the Thursday, his friends hired a room where they could eat the Passover meal with Jesus. Judas came to the meal, but left early.

Afterwards, Jesus went with his friends into a garden called Gethsemane. Soon Judas arrived with some armed men who took Jesus away.

First Jesus was tried by a religious court who said he had broken God's laws by calling himself the Son of God. The punishment for this was death, but no one was allowed to kill him without permission from the Romans, who ruled the country.

So the next day Jesus was tried again by the Roman governor, Pontius Pilate, who would not interfere and allowed Jesus to be punished.

Then, Jesus was taken to a place called Golgotha and crucified. At the end of the day, when he was dead, his body was put in a tomb and a big stone was rolled in front.

On that Sunday a woman called Mary Magdalene went to the tomb, only to find the stone had been rolled away, and the body of Jesus was gone. Two angels were there. They told her that Jesus had risen from the dead.

There are many stories of people seeing Jesus after he had risen from the dead. After this, Jesus' friends traveled about the world, preaching the new religion.

# Index

# Answers

You will find the answers to the quiz on these pages:

Question     1: page 5
2: page 21
3: page 38
4: page 44
5: page 10
6: page 11

DUE DAT